D1272661

ON THE PLACE OF
GILBERT CHESTERTON
IN
ENGLISH LETTERS

By

HILAIRE BELLOC

With an Introductory Essay

by

DOUGLAS WOODRUFF

PATMOS PRESS

SHEPHERDSTOWN, WEST VIRGINIA

1977

Printed in The United States of America

To
MAURICE BARING

Introductory Essay © 1977 by Patmos Press, Inc.
First Published in 1940 by Sheed and Ward,
    London and New York
Library of Congress Catalog Card Number: 76–40399
ISBN: 0–915762–04–8

MY DEAR MAURICE,

I have taken the liberty of using your name in connection with this very short preface to my very short study upon our common friend Gilbert Chesterton. I am sure your name ought to be connected with any memory of his, so greatly did he admire your work and so much do you stand for what you and I and he had in common by the end of our various pilgrimages. We share, I believe, also a common and deep respect for his memory.

There is much in these few pages which I am sure you will hardly agree with, and here and there sentences with which you will perhaps actively disagree, but I know that he would have been proud and honoured to have your name coupled with his even in so brief and imperfect an appreciation as this.

H. BELLOC

Kings Land,
    Shipley,
        Sussex.
August 1940

BELLOC'S INFLUENCE
ON CHESTERTON

BY

DOUGLAS WOODRUFF

It will not escape the reader's notice that Belloc's essay on *The Place of Gilbert Chesterton in English Letters* is a misnomer for what follows which is much more an appreciation of Chesterton's place in the public life of England. Belloc was persuaded to write this appreciation by Frank and Maisie Sheed, when Belloc had made it definitely clear that however often they asked him he was not going to write an autobiography or reminiscences, the kind of book in which he would naturally have written about Chesterton just as Chesterton had devoted a whole chapter of his own autobiography called "Portrait of a Friend" to Belloc. The nearest thing Belloc came to autobiography was *The Cruise of the "Nona"* of 1925, in which Chesterton does not appear. I recall that I was myself a little shocked when at Chesterton's funeral I saw Belloc booking himself to write as many appreciations as he could get commissioned, and I made some remark about the number, to which he replied briefly "They can all be different." In fact, he made over and over again the same point that Chesterton was fundamentally and seriously concerned for the public good, that he cared much more about the effect of what he had to say than about gaining admiration or reward

I

for the way in which he said it. This would have pleased Chesterton, who always insisted that he was, by vocation a journalist, a man writing for his own day, and indifferent to posthumous reputation. When he surveyed the allegorical tales rather misleadingly called novels, with which he had first become prominent as a man of letters, he concluded that they all contained important ideas which he had failed to work out as effectively as they deserved; and that he had failed because he had not taken the immense pains novelists must take, and had not taken the pains because he was a journalist first and last, a man of articles rather than of books. Belloc, too, was a journalist, but he never prided himself upon the way of life into which he had drifted after waiting for four years for a teaching appointment in Oxford, and never securing anything better than extra-mural extension lecturing, which meant long and tedious train journeys round the cities of the industrial north.

So it was altogether suitable that the two men originally met when they were both contributing to the same weekly paper, *The Speaker*. This was a weekly founded and written by young Oxford Liberals, edited by one of them, J. L. Hammond, who afterwards became so valued by C. P. Scott of the *Manchester Guardian* that Scott entrusted him with the editorship when he himself took one of his rare holidays. Two of the Oxford contributors, Edmund Bentley and Lucian Oldershaw, had been Chesterton's closest intimates as school boys at St. Paul's, the great London day school. They had been members of the Junior Debating Club in which Chesterton had developed what was to remain his lifelong style as a journalist, a style better suited to the spoken than to the written word, designed to arrest and hold the listener's attention by startling paradox constantly embellished with punning and playing on words. It proved highly effective in newspaper journalism, stood up less well when the articles were collected in book form, and it was, incidentally, a style that jarred on Belloc, with his classical approach to the writing of prose, as the reader of his essay will note.

It was Bentley, as he himself told me, who had been responsible for Chesterton not going to Oxford. Bentley, already an undergraduate, had persuaded Chesterton's parents that he would be likely to be given a very bad time, as often happened to clever boys from the day schools of London and other big cities when they encountered the unintellectual public school "hearties" who predominated and set the tone in the Oxford of the 'nineties. Chesterton as a youth looked very odd. It was his wife, as he gladly admitted, who invented the draped figure with whom the world became so well acquainted. Chesterton went instead to art school in London, the Slade, and so he never knew the intellectual rigour of the Oxford tutorial system, with the tutor taking apart every sentence of the undergraduate's weekly essay. As an art student he read widely in English literature, but he did not read history. Yet it was historical knowledge that formed the armament of the political journalist, and he has left a record of the impression Belloc made on him at their first meeting. Bentley and Oldershaw having introduced him to *The Speaker* as another lively pen with the same ardent pro-Boer or anti-Imperialist sentiments, took him to meet their Oxford friend, Belloc, at a Soho restaurant. Belloc was talking about King John, how he was not the best king England had known because he had been regent, and there was no instance where a man who had been regent made a good king. Chesterton remarked that he, for one, had not come equipped with a list of regents who had made good kings, and obviously did not know that in English medieval history John is the only king who was regent, so there was really no substance to what Belloc was saying. But it was the meeting of a man whose mind ran naturally on history with one whose mind ran naturally on literature. All his life Belloc talked disparagingly of books that were about other books, admitted that he was himself a bad reviewer. Although, through his Oxford friend, the son of the proprietor of *The Morning Post* he became the literary editor of that arch-Conservative journal while sitting as a Radical in Parliament, he was not a good literary editor. He kept the position for a number of years because of the excellence of the weekly essays he himself contributed, which the paper would have lost. The manager constantly remonstrated at the unremitting hostility towards and mockery of the rich whom *The Morning Post* regarded as its essential public. Belloc always replied that the rich would stand anything except being bored, and did not mind being attacked, provided they were interested and amused.

We come here to the basis of the friendship formed during the Boer War between Belloc and Chesterton. It was an alliance against the immensely powerful plutocracy of late Victorian and Edwardian England. Belloc had been born in 1870, Chesterton in 1874. The one was forty-four, the other forty when the Great War of 1914 brought to an end the world in which they had grown up and in which their minds had been formed. Chesterton died in 1936 without ever realising that the enemy against whom he had pitted himself since boyhood was no longer in command, and Belloc, although he lived till 1953, lost his intellectual grasp after a stroke in 1941, and in the last twelve years of his life was vague and detached about the outside world. In the last year of his life, when the Abyssinian War broke out, Chesterton minded very much more about the activities of an English financier called Ricketts who was seeking oil concessions in Abyssinia than about Mussolini who was invading and annexing that country. Chesterton was like an old war-horse scenting the battle when he heard about Ricketts, and exclaimed "Here is my old enemy!" and felt he was back facing the financiers in whose interests the agricultural settlements of the pastoral Boers had been annexed by the British Empire as soon as gold and diamonds were found under their soil.

This belief that the enemies were the rich was highly personal with Belloc. When he knew that I would be writing about him after his death, he told me several things which he wanted understood. He was, for example, insistent that it was a complete misunderstanding to think that it was his French blood which had made him a rebel. The misunderstanding came about because his first serious books were laudatory biographies of Danton and Robespierre. He had wanted to write about English history, and in particular about his central thesis that the key to an understanding of modern England was the successful seizure by the landed gentry, chiefly new men, of the church lands which Henry VIII had appropriated to the Crown, but had then been unable to retain. The publishers took the line that the English Reformation was overtrodden ground: it was French history that needed to be better understood, and that Belloc, a French citizen with an Oxford training, was the man to do it. A Frenchman, Belloc insisted, is not naturally a rebel, the Revolution was soon ended with them all enthusiastically serving a new master, the Emperor Napoleon, for a Frenchman's instinct, when he sees something strong, is to join it. It was his Irish blood from an Irish family that settled in France in the eighteenth century and produced the mother of his French father, that made him a rebel. But it was also very important that when he was about sixteen his mother had lost what little money she had through entrusting it to a stockbroker who lodged in her house in Wimpole Street. He went on to explain that his sister, two years his senior, shared the horrible secret with her mother, but that it was kept from the boy. All he knew was that there was a sudden change of demeanour, that his mother and sister suddenly took to saying: "Here comes a rich person, Hilary. Get down on all fours!" He had resented this and had not complied. He had made rich friends at the Oratory School, but he left at sixteen.

There followed six years between school and university in which he had grown to democratic manhood, walking the whole length of the United States from Philadelphia, where he had distant kinsfolk, to California, the home of the Irish-American girl whom he was pursuing, and did eventually marry. They were six years during which he mixed with the new society that was forming in the American Middle West, and its democratic influence was reinforced when he became a driver in the French Artillery for ten formative months in his twentieth year, the ten months being the shorter period allowed to conscripts who were, as he was, the only son of a widow. His sister had been the secretary of the celebrated Radical editor, W. T. Stead, and she had persuaded Stead to give her young brother a few francs to visit the French provinces on an old penny-farthing bicycle and send back impressions of provincial France. This was before he did his military service, and it played its part in making him want to see more of the ordinary Frenchman, the peasant-proprietors, who made the strength of the nation and had no counterpart in late Victorian England.

He had tried to help the dockers in the famous dock strike of 1889, and had visited Cardinal Manning as often, he said, as the Cardinal would receive him, and they talked of the injustices suffered by the poor, and the indifference of the old English Catholic families to social questions. He had experienced in his own person the conflict between the claims of liberty, which leads to great inequality, and the claims of the poor whom only the State could assist quickly and effectively. When I once asked him who had impressed him most among his elders, he did not say Manning but Gladstone. Yet Gladstone, even in that last phase when Belloc could hear him speak, and he was coming to be called "The Peoples William", was much more concerned with liberty than with radical reform, and maintained to the end a profound dislike of Government expenditure, and very appropriately closed his active career by resigning over the naval estimates which were the first national response to the announced intention of the new German Empire to build such a navy as should be able, one day, to challenge the world-wide supremacy of the British Navy. Gladstone's greatest merit in Belloc's eyes had not been his public thrift or his championing of a free society, with the money of its citizens being left to fructify in the pockets of the people, but in his grasping the Irish nettle and attempting to give the Irish Home Rule. The attempt was defeated by the House of Lords, many of whose more wealthy members owned vast estates in Ireland, and this defeat of Home Rule while Belloc was still at Oxford, making his name as a young Radical, was personified in the person of Joseph Chamberlain.

The Chamberlains were Birmingham Unitarians with no aristocratic pretensions, distantly connected with Belloc's own Birmingham Unitarian grandfather, Joseph Parkes, who had married the granddaughter of the most famous of all Birmingham Unitarians before Joseph Chamberlain, Joseph Priestley. Belloc had been christened Joseph after his grandfather, but not without a backward glance to that great-great-grandfather. Joseph Chamberlain had been the great Radical leader until the Home Rule issue was raised, when he broke with Gladstone and led a Liberal-Unionist Party into alliance with the Conservatives. When the Conservatives came to power after Gladstone's withdrawal and Rosebery's defeat in the election of 1895, Chamberlain asked for the Colonial Office. This was a highly unusual choice, for it had never ranked as one of the chief Cabinet posts. Yet Chamberlain, the second man in the Government after Lord Salisbury, chose it as the office from which he could best promote the imperial idea. It was no accident that the Colonial Office had ranked so low in the hierarchy of Cabinet posts. The colonies ranked even lower in the thinking and practice of the City of London. Nineteenth century London, as the financial capital of the world, treated the whole globe as its field for investment. It was just as interested in developing the United States or Central or South America, or financing railways in Central Europe as it was in the colonies, by which then were principally meant the countries settled from England, Canada, Australia, New Zealand. The colonial conferences which began to be held from 1887 were attended by those White Dominions while the Colonial Secretary directly represented the colonies proper, governed from London, chiefly in Africa, but scattered round the globe. All these colonies together did not strike the imagination of Englishmen as much as their Indian Empire for which the Queen had received in 1877 the title of Empress of India by Disraeli. Until the East India Company was wound up so that India should be directly ruled through a Viceroy responsible to the Secretary of State for India, East India House had been a great landmark for over two centuries in Leadenhall Street. The fact that India was not part of the Colonial Office greatly diminished the status of the Colonial Secretary. He was not the main, only the second, Cabinet Minister with imperial responsibilities.

Chamberlain assumed office in 1895, and in the next year the Jameson Raid, the abortive attempt to seize power in the Boer Republics, began the South African crisis. In 1898 Belloc published *The Modern Traveller,* a narrative poem which has retained its high comic quality, a satire on the new type of cosmopolitan financier engaged in developing trade with tropical Africa. The Boers would not grant votes to all the adventurers who had streamed into their quiet pastoral republics as soon as diamonds and gold were discovered, because they feared they would be swamped by the newcomers with their wealth and ruthless exploitation of great riches under the soil. But Cecil Rhodes, a clergyman's son from England, who had made a great fortune in the gold and diamond rush and had become Prime Minister of the British Cape Colony, was looking north to extend the Empire with the foundation of Rhodesia, and the Boer republics lay across his path. It was resolved to annex them, thus giving security under the British flag to the gold and diamond interests. There had been many colonial wars in the century which had not aroused any public feeling in England, but the Boer War, technically the Third Boer War, aroused immense hostility. It threatened to split the Liberal Party into Imperialists and pro-Boers. The men who were to head the great Liberal Government which was to govern England for almost ten years, from the end of 1905 until May 1915,

Asquith, Haldane and Grey, were Imperialists, supporting the war. But the majority of Liberals who found their spokesman in the emerging figure of Lloyd George, were pro-Boers, and it was to this wing of the Party that Belloc, Chesterton and Gilbert's younger brother, Cecil, devoted themselves, passing from *The Speaker* to write in the Radical *Daily News*.

For Chesterton it was a far cry from the life at arts school where he had developed his remarkable gift for drawing men, imaginary, and slightly absurd men, and the life of literary criticism, where he had steeped himself in English literature, past and present. He has left a record of the impression Belloc made on him as a thinker and writer who was also a man of action. Chesterton lived in the mind, but he did not fail to notice how many other Radicals did the same. They might sing "The Red Flag", and he would sing it with them, or Blake's "Jerusalem", but these songs assumed victory. They gave no hint of how victory was to be achieved. Belloc won Chesterton's admiration as a practical campaigner, and Chesterton particularly liked Belloc's violent poem "The Rebel" because it was also a description of military tactics. It was in keeping with both men's characters that Belloc should seek to enter and succeed in entering the House of Commons, sitting for an industrial Manchester seat with a high proportion of Catholic voters. It never crossed Chesterton's mind, nor anybody else's, that he should become an M.P. When Belloc ruined his prospects in the Liberal Party, as he quickly did, with one unfortunate phrase about the Anglo-Judaic Plutocracy, and by demanding an audit of the Party funds, those Party funds were naturally refused him when a General Election came in 1910. He fought and held the seat at his own expense. But when there was a second election in the same year he would not face the expense again, withdrew from Parliament, and for the rest of his life continued to deride it, declaring that the humblest voice in the smallest newspaper was worth more than the right to speak and vote in an assembly that was not free.

The end of his parliamentary career corresponded with the beginning of the Welfare State. Lloyd George introduced compulsory National Insurance against unemployment and ill-health. It did nothing to recommend these measures that they were modelled on laws long established in Prussia by Bismarck.

The introduction of Labour Exchanges and the quite modest but compulsory weekly stamps to be bought by both employers and employees in order to provide a fund for unemployment benefit and a rudimentary health service, were enough to convince Belloc that he had detected a new and very sinister plan by which the rich could control and exploit the poor. He published *The Servile State* in 1912 after quarrelling violently with Charles Masterman who was his friend and Chesterton's on *The Daily News*. Masterman was an ambitious Member of Parliament and in 1909 accepted

minor office to help Lloyd George with his new poli-
cies. The rule then was that when a Member of Parliament accepted Cabinet office he had to resign his
seat and offer himself for re-election. In 1913 Belloc
felt so strongly against Masterman that he went down
to the constituency in East London and opened com-
mittee rooms to work for Masterman's defeat. The
Government had been in office over seven years, and
had earned a good deal of unpopularity, and was
losing its by-elections. Masterman was defeated, and it
proved the end of his brief ministerial career. Belloc
exulted, but Chesterton, in 1912, dedicated his chal-
lenging book *What's wrong with the World?* to
Masterman and maintained the friendship. But he
subscribed wholeheartedly to the thesis of *The Servile
State*. When he was writing his autobiography in what
proved to be the last year of his life, 1935 to 1936,
he re-stated the thesis of *The Servile State* because,
he claimed, Belloc had often been misunderstood.
Chesterton then set out what he understood Belloc to
be saying, making it plain that he believed the thesis to
be both true and important. The thesis was quite
simply that what was called the capturing and en-
registering of the proletariate was being done by
capitalists with Lloyd George—commonly called by
Belloc "the man George"—as their conscious agent.
The mass of men were to be made to work for the
benefit of a small rich class which alone would enjoy
liberty as well as the other pleasures of a high stan-

dard of living. We can see today what a mythical picture this was. The working classes are very closely controlled by their Trade Unions, less closely by the State. The Trade Unions hold their members' livelihoods in their hands, for if they expel a man who practises a skilled trade the result can be ruinous, and as the unions succeed in extending the principle of the closed shop, by which employers undertake not to employ anybody who is not a member of the union concerned, to fall foul of the union is the risk few members ever dare to run. Thanks to the secret ballot a third of the Trade Union membership can and does refuse to vote for the Labour Party which the Trade Unions themselves created at the beginning of the century. But in all industrial matters the demarcation of the frontiers between jobs, how hard a man shall work, when and for what reason he shall strike, the Trade Unionist often vote with a show of hands. But it requires great courage to go against the wishes of the shop stewards, the Union officials in a man's place of work.

Next to the Trade Unions the control of State bureaucracy confines and limits the liberty of the ordinary man. Local authorities lay down the law for the tenants of their council houses in much greater detail than private landlords have ever dared to do. They insist on how the garden should be maintained, or that no dogs or cats shall be kept. Because the rents of council houses are less than those on the open market, tenants who may have waited for years to get a council house, are very afraid of being dispossessed. Belloc was quite right in foreseeing a steady diminution in the freedom of choice left the ordinary weekly wage-earner, but he was wildly wrong in connecting this development with the interests of a small, rich class. He was a man of forty-four when the old world and the Edwardian plutocracy came to an end. Very few people recognised the form the war of 1914 was going to take, the immense carnage and the way in which it would be necessary to keep up the morale of the population by promising that all the sacrifices would lead to something much more than the defeat of the Kaiser and his armies. They were to lead a new Britain, an immense leap forward in the standard of living of the working classes. Every effort was made after the war to restore the world as Englishmen had known it before 1914. But it could not be done. But when the war ended Belloc was nearly fifty and thoroughly set in his ways. He had taught his young children that when reproved by strangers, the only answer they would ever need to make was "My father is richer than you."

When I first met him in 1920, he said that poverty had descended upon him so that he could no longer afford his two boats and his motor-car. He went on to say how much he regretted that he had not gone to the Chancery Bar of which his English grandfather had been the historian. With his immense powers of concentrated work and brilliant exposition, I think

there can be no doubt he would have acquired a very
large practice and a very large income. But he said
when you were young you liked the acclaim that went
with writing, not pausing to reflect how the writer's
career can leave you stranded in middle life with your
name well-known but your income small and precari-
ous, only achieved with an effort that grows ever
more irksome, as the creative powers lessen. One of
the pleasant fruits of early literary success was that
you were a welcome guest in great houses, and Belloc,
from his Oxford days, had always had a number of
such houses to welcome him. He was such good
friends with the Astors in spite of Nancy Astor's deep-
rooted antipathy to Belloc's religion as well as to his
love of wine, that when his wife died, she took his
young family into her great Thames-side home at
Cliveden. But his contact with the high life of England inevitably diminished as he grew older, although
he always had a number of country hostesses to whom
he paid his restless visits. While he appreciated this
hospitality, it continually underlined the contrast between the way the rich with secure incomes were able
to live and the life of the harrassed, insecure writer
living from one publisher's commission to the next,
and knowing he could not afford to be ill or to leave
off writing. It remains very strange, all the same, that
he should have continued throughout the inter-war
period so to exaggerate the power of the rich in political life, when it was in fact diminishing all the time.

What is surprising about Chesterton's attitude to the rich is that for all his great good nature and wide charity, he continued to write so fiercely against them. There was nothing parallel to Belloc's personal experience. Born into a comfortable, middle-class family with a good estate-agents' business, which is still flourishing in the West End of London, he had a father who could make him an allowance when he set out to live by his pen. When he married at twenty-six, in the year in which he met Belloc, he left home for the first time, and started his married life in a flat in Battersea, on which Belloc wrote a poem which began:

> Gilbert and Frances have a little flat
> At eighty pounds a year, and cheap at that.

He never frequented the houses of the rich, or went anywhere without his wife. He never made very much money and was generous with what he had, so that in the last ten years of his life he relied on his very capable young secretary, Dorothy Collins, to tell him when the bank balance had sunk to the danger-mark which he placed around a hundred pounds. When that figure was reached he would find the remedy by writing another "Father Brown" story, the most highly-rewarded form of writing which he practised. After his brother's death in 1918 he was the only child. His father died in 1921, his mother in 1933, which left him better-off for the last two years of his life. He seems never to have questioned the thesis of

INTRODUCTION

The Servile State, accepted Belloc's view of the politicians as the self-seeking and corrupt agents of finance
capitalism, enjoyed writing rhetorically about the
barricades, and he was nearly fifty when he wrote his
wellknown poem

> Laugh at us, pay us, pass us,
> But do not quite forget
> That we are the people of England
> Who never have spoken yet.

The poem contains a lightning survey of English history, with the English people silent under mis-govern-
ment, watching the destruction of the monasteries,
those "Inns of God where no man paid", treating the
English Civil War as a conflict between two groups
of the rich, ending in 1688 in the final triumph of the
rich, landed oligarchy over the King, who might have
acted for the common people. The Napoleonic War
was seen as one in which the people of England
"strove and fought like lions to keep ourselves in
chains." And then there followed the rise of the plutocracy with the golden age of the Victorian company
directors, largely the "little jewelled alien men" of
another of his poems. Finally the people of England say

> It may be we shall rise the last
> As France rose up the first,
> Our wrath come after Russia's wrath,
> And our wrath be the worst.

INTRODUCTION

As though any sane man could treat Lenin and Trotsky's seizure of power and exploitation of the war-weariness of the long-suffering Russian people as representing "Russia's wrath." But equally, and this was very Chestertonian—the people of England admitted that it might well be that they would not rise but would go on with the comfortable philosophy that "beer is best."

Chesterton always maintained that the correct balance a man should keep was ferocity in his intellectual opinions combined with amiability in his personal relations. Like theologians who tell us to hate the sin but to love the sinner, Chesterton saw himself as hating bad opinions but not hating the men who held them. Perhaps he did not hate the individuals he knew, and he was not a good hater, but it cannot be pretended that he attacked ideas and not men. One poem ends

> And those who rule in England
> In solemn conclave met.
> Alas, alas for England,
> They have no graves as yet.

Yet I remember his expressing to me his disappointment that when he had met Stanley Baldwin at Lord Desborough's home, Taplow Court, which was very near Chesterton's own modest home at Beaconsfield, Baldwin had not been at all genial towards him. Chesterton thought they had a great deal in common, as

Englishmen with a love of rural England, but to Baldwin Chesterton was the accomplice of Belloc in a continual subversive denigration of those who carried the heavy burden of the public business of the nation.

While Belloc and Chesterton were Radicals in the sense that their prescription for the health of England went to the root of the diseases in the social order, they were never regarded as Radicals by the other Radicals, the much more numerous and vociferous advocates of more state control with whom the future lay. To these men medieval was one of the most pejorative adjectives in the language, the Middle Ages even worse than the first phase of the Industrial Revolution; a time when the common man suffered oppression, poverty and disease, only slightly mitigated by the comforts which also brought their own terrors of gross superstition. When Belloc and Chesterton called for wider distribution of private property they did so in a context of Back to the Land. This did not make much appeal to the vast urban population who wanted more free services from the Government as well as more money from their employers. Belloc had derived his idea of a free peasantry from provincial France as he had seen it in his boyhood with peasant proprietors who were very little hampered by government regulations. But through the first half of the twentieth century British Governments concerned themselves more and more with regulating agricultural production. The poultry farmer, the pig farmer, the man with a few cows, all found themselves brought under a discipline of marketing-boards and Government regulations as well as the looming presence of the large companies to whom most of them had to sell their products if they wanted any security for their output. While Belloc wrote about the re-distribution of property in his most practical and expository manner, both he and Chesterton had written so much and so eloquently about the Middle Ages that it did not call for very much misrepresentation or mental confusion for people to think that their programme was a romantic call to go back to a highly imaginary Merry England; and there were few takers. Secularist and socialist radicals were not prepared to believe that Roman Catholics could be anything but reactionary. Inside the growing Labour movement the secularists were gaining, decade by decade, against the Nonconformists. Originally the Labour Party owed a great deal to the strong Nonconformity especially of the north of England. Its first secretary, Arthur Henderson, had been a Wesleyan lay-preacher, but Nonconformists were Christians with an inherited profound mistrust of the Church of Rome and all its ways. To the secularists like Ramsay Macdonald, the first Labour Prime Minister, the Roman Catholic Church was an integral part of the established order which Socialism was destined to supplant. A man who became a Catholic as Chesterton did, deliberately, in

middle life, might write as much as he liked about the
barricades and the people of England, but he would
not be believed by those who were working for a new
kind of society based on a vast extension of state bene-
fits and state interference with all economic life.

In the essay that follows Belloc refers to a very
curious conversation with Chesterton when Chesterton
was trying to explain his continuing hesitation about
entering the Church. He wanted, he said, to find some-
one who was thoroughly English in blood and outlook
and who yet had made his submission to Rome. He
excluded his two close friends, Belloc and Maurice
Baring for their French or Jewish blood. It is very
odd that he should have overlooked Aubrey Herbert,
Lord Lucas. Lucas had been Minister of Agriculture
and the only Catholic in the Asquith Liberal Government after the resignation of the aged Lord Ripon. He
had been killed as a Royal Flying Corps pilot early in
the war. He had, incidentally, bequeathed four thousand pounds to Belloc and a thousand pounds to Chesterton. If a later convert with no foreign blood was
needed, the distinguished Anglican, Ronald Knox, had
been received in 1917. It is difficult to think that
Chesterton was doing more than make a poor excuse
for having dawdled for so long on a journey he knew
he had to take. Belloc used to say that as far back as
1905 Chesterton had assured him he was going to be
received before the end of the year, and his younger
brother, Cecil, had been received in 1909 when he was

thirty. Belloc admired Cecil as a man of decision and resolution, superior to his brother in those respects, and said that Gilbert had been afraid of his wife and anxious not to distress his ageing Unitarian father, and this is supported by the fact that Chesterton did wait until his father died before asking his Irish friend, Monsignor O'Connor, to receive him. His wife followed him shortly afterwards, and in 1926 it was she who was responsible for finding for her husband the resident secretary who was also a Catholic and who became a third invaluable member of the household. Chesterton's mind had crystallised, he said, when he had visited Jerusalem to write the book *The New Jerusalem* which had appeared in 1920. His Zionist sympathies were limited, and it might be said fairly enough that for him one of the great attractions in the British Government's policy of providing a national home for the Jews in part of what had been the Ottoman Empire, was that it carried a tacit acknowledgement that the Jews were a race, distinct from the English, a nomadic people everywhere. It was for this very reason that a great many Jews have always opposed Zionism because it cuts across their claim to be thoroughly English or American or French, only differing from other citizens by their religion. When Chesterton asked Maurice Baring, who had influential friends, to obtain for him a passport to Palestine, he stated his purpose as the writing of what he called semi-historical rhetoric. From a reviewer's pen the expression would have been belittling, but it was Chesterton's own, and shows his modest view of the various volumes of impressions which he wrote at the invitation of publishers or editors, covering, in addition to Palestine, Ireland, the United States and Italy. Whereas Belloc had been an inveterate and tireless traveller from his teens, and wrote that he could not imagine any man being so poor that he could not travel, Chesterton was a stay-at-home who never went far afield until invited in his public capacity either to lecture or to write. He was not only what was termed a "Little Englander" in his ideas but also in his personal life, which may help to explain that strange conversation about looking for other wholly English converts, as though nationality could have any relevance in face of the claims of the Universal or Catholic Church.

The friendship between Belloc and Chesterton gave Chesterton much more than it gave Belloc. It was an education for Chesterton in its first phase when it can be clearly seen that it was Belloc's influence, combined with that of his younger brother, Cecil, that turned him against the Liberal Party. He considered himself a good party man as late as the Liberal landslide victory in 1906 which carried other Liberal journalists like Charles Masterman into the House of Commons as well as Belloc. There are enough books by Belloc written before he renounced his French nationality in order to sit in the Commons to show that he had no great illusions, although it is difficult to credit the assertion he was fond of making later, that he had only entered Parliament to get more publicity for his books. But Gilbert Chesterton was writing in 1908 that while his faith in Liberalism was as strong as ever, there had been a rosy time of innocence when he had believed in Liberals.

In this first phase the Chesterton brothers and Belloc were constantly together, all writing for Fleet Street papers and meeting and drinking in Fleet Street pubs. While they wrote praise of wine, and Belloc never liked whisky, the Chesterton brothers did, to the point that Mrs. Chesterton took the firm decision that Gilbert should leave London for what was then the small Buckinghamshire town of Beaconsfield, some 30 miles from London, and this was undoubtedly a wise step which prolonged his life and activity. But Mrs. Chesterton was not very encouraging towards her husband's London friends, and in the second phase, from the departure to Beaconsfield in 1908 until Chesterton's reception into the Church, Belloc saw less of him. They saw more of each other, still not a great deal, in the final phase between Chesterton's conversion in 1922 and his death fourteen years later in June, 1936.

Belloc, after the 1914 war in which his weekly extensive war commentary had preoccupied him, entered on the second phase of his literary career as a preeminently Catholic writer. The change was signallised by the publication of *Europe and the Faith* in 1920. He began to acquire an American public, such as he had not known in his great creative period before 1914. In the '20's and '30's, as American Catholic universities discovered his gifts as a lecturer, he came more and more to rely upon this new market, and to take more part in the life of English Catholicism where Chesterton also was in great demand. Belloc's novels which Chesterton illustrated for him, drawing as many as a dozen pictures in an afternoon, became known as the "Chester-Bellocs" adopting a nickname which Bernard Shaw had coined much earlier to express the close relationship, much as Shaw deplored the great influence Belloc exercised over a man whom Shaw greatly cherished. Belloc, who was always complaining that most of the national press was closed to him, wrote frequently for *G.K.'s Weekly,* and took over the editorship when Chesterton died, to pave the way for his son-in-law, Reginald Jebb, a convert and a convinced Distributist. Under him *G.K.'s Weekly* changed its name to *The Weekly Review* which lasted into, but did not survive, the Second World War. Belloc always maintained that Chesterton's reputation would have grown very much more slowly if he had had to carry the burdensome label of Roman Catholicism from the beginning of his writing career, that the Anglicans had given him a great welcome as a Christian apologist who was one of themselves. Certainly it was very widely said outside the Catholic body that Chesterton ceased to write so well after his conversion. Old Mr. Cox of the London Library, when readers asked for a book by Chesterton, never failed to make the remark. It is a difficult criticism to sustain, for *The Everlasting Man* ranks very high in Chesterton's output, and it was the first fruits of his conversion. Its climax, the great contrast between the strangeness of the Christian revelation and the sanity and balance of the resulting society when European men had accepted the guidance of that revelation as mediated to them through the Catholic Church, ends with a picture of happy boyhood which could not conceivably be applied to the Scottish Kirk, so that although *The Everlasting Man,* in its broad sweep, is a Christian apologetic, it is Catholic Christianity that is implied. Chesterton demonstrates first the uniqueness of man in the animal creation, and then the uniqueness of Christ in human history, the supernatural revelation bringing, almost as a by-product, the highest civilisation for the natural man. Evelyn Waugh was so impressed with the massive argument, and so repelled by the verbal mannerisms of Chesterton's style, that he seriously contemplated asking the author's leave to re-state his argument in economical, classical, and precise prose, and I have little doubt that Chesterton, in his humility and apostolicity would have readily agreed.

What those who said that he did not write so well after his conversion had in their minds was that he became much more predictable, and that the paradoxical style was much better suited to unpredictability; that when he had first burst upon the world with his verbal fireworks, the conclusions were likely to be as startling as the form as he challenged common assumptions and widespread prejudices. But as he said, the great point of an open mind was that one day it could close upon firm convictions. A man should start life with an open mind but it would be a sad story if, after all his exploration and reciptivity, he never found what he was seeking. It was Chesterton's happiness that he did. "Prove all things: hold fast to that which is true."

Belloc would have understood what Evelyn Waugh meant, as he says in this essay: "It would have been better perhaps had Chesterton never fallen into verbalism (wherein he tended to exceed). For fools were led thereby to think that he was merely verbalist, whereas he was, in reality, a thinker so profound and so direct that he had no equal."

ON THE PLACE OF
GILBERT CHESTERTON
IN
ENGLISH LETTERS

WHAT follows are the notes of a friend (but an intimate friend) on a great contemporary writer.

I attempt no panegyric, nor even an analysis of Gilbert Chesterton's writings. No doubt I exaggerate some aspects of Chesterton's character and literary action; I also know too little about other aspects of his life and work.

Thus I have no full familiarity with the Church of England in its domestic and intimate character, and I have had few relations with the Anglican Clergy. Chesterton during all the middle part of his life was in close touch with the Establishment, and he and his wife were particular friends and intimates of more than one distinguished

Anglican clergyman. But the family tradition in which I was born and by which I was moulded in early years was, socially, of the Birmingham Unitarian world from which my English family derived. It was by this world, its literature and moral habit, that I was surrounded in those* early years when character is formed, and we inherited much of our domestic atmosphere from the memory of that illustrious man of Science, Dr. Joseph Priestly whose portraits on the walls of the house are part of my surroundings. Now Gilbert Chesterton came also in early youth under the Unitarian influence. We were both of us acquainted with the spirit.

But my chief claim to know and interpret Chesterton is, of course, a permanent and active personal friendship, through which we were very close companions for

* My mother was received into the Catholic Church four years before I was born. Her approach to the Faith was through the intelligence.

more than 30 years and during nearly the whole of his literary activity. We collaborated in the long series of weekly literary work beginning with the *Eye Witness,* which I founded in 1911 and the editorship of which his brother Cecil Chesterton, took on in the following year.

Between us we were instrumental in exposing the Marconi scandal. Both before I went into Parliament, and while I was in the House of Commons, I had ample opportunity for observing the rapid decline of public life through its unchecked corruption, the mark of which was (and still is) the strange absence of public discussion thereon. But the thing was equally apparent to men who were free from the business of Westminster and no one was clearer in vision or harder in action during the vain struggle for purity in public life than these two brothers.

It is now too late to set things right in

this department; the Parliamentary profession in England, despite its long national tradition, has lost its former vigour and respect. It will linger on indefinitely as a form, but is now rarely of vital effect upon public affairs. These are now almost openly controlled by the great monopolies, especially those of the banking system, and comment upon political speeches and votes has become futile.

Recognising this as he did, Gilbert Chesterton turned more and more to the two living activities which should most occupy serious attention: social philosophy and religion.

In the former field, he grew more and more definite in his attitude. He defended the common man and his freedom; therefore he defended the institution of property and particularly defended and preached the doctrine that property to survive must be founded on so considerable a division of land and the instruments of production that widespread ownership should be the foundational institution of the state. He appreciated, of course, as all must, the immense difficulty in re-establishing property in a society which has become, as ours has, proletarian and controlled in every activity by an ever-narrowing plutocracy. He saw that the weapon to be used against this mortal state of affairs was perpetual influence by illustration and example upon the individual. It was his to change as far as might be the very lethargic mind of his fellow-citizens in these affairs. This political preoccupation of Gilbert Chesterton's was of special importance because it is the major temporal concern of our time.

The group to which he and I belonged recognised that the main social event of our generation was the destruction of freedom through the universal growth of Capitalist monopoly, and the ruin of economic independence in the mass of private citizens.

Perhaps the evil has so established itself in England as to be beyond remedy. Certainly our contemporaries so regard it. All affirm that the revival of freedom among Englishmen is now past praying for. They must consent to living as dependants upon a small class which controls the very means of livelihood and therefore life itself. Nowhere is this control more apparent than in the English Press, which has sunk beyond that of any other public instrument of information in Christendom, and has become a mere commercial dependence upon Big Business.

It is essential to a comprehension of Gilbert Chesterton's life, even in the field of literature (which stands half apart today from politics), to understand that this *political* aim to which he and I and all our group were vowed, the Restoration of Property, the struggle against Communism and the Capitalism whence Communism springs, was our (and his) chief temporal aim. It may be a forlorn hope but it is by far the most outstanding of public efforts in the ruined society of our day; and for all our isolation and presumable failure, posterity will note that a little body wherein he was so conspicuous, still defended the cause of the free family and of the man master of himself in his own home.

But such a temporal object must, like all external worldly objects, depend upon an underlying internal spirit. Only a philosophy can produce political action and a philosophy is only vital when it is the soul of a religion.

Now here we come to the thing of chief value and of chief effect in Gilbert Chesterton's life and work: his religion. In this department I have a task quite different from the common appreciation of literary style and matter. From a man's religion (or accepted and certain philosophy) all his actions spring, whether he be conscious of that connection or no. In the case of Gilbert Chesterton, the whole of whose expression and action were the story of a life's religion, the connection was not only evident to himself but to all around, and even to the general public. That public of modern England, has been taught universally that religion is at once a private personal affair and of little external effect. Our public is more agreed upon religion, and less acquainted with its diverse and multitudinous actions, than any other in the modern world; but even so all those who know anything of him, even if it be but his name, are aware of that great accident (or design) whereby he advanced towards the Faith over many years and was ultimately in full communion with it.

He approached the Catholic Church gradually but by a direct road. He first saw the city from afar off, then approached it

with interest and at last entered. Few of
the great conversions in our history have
been so deliberate or so mature. It will be
for posterity to judge the magnitude of the
event. We are too near it to see it in scale.
It may be that England will soon lose what
fragment it retains of the Creed which
made Europe, and by the survival of which
may Europe survive. It may be just the
other way: England may be passing
through a crisis and turning point in this
matter and may be destined to recover by
some unexpected return of fate the influence which brought the nation into being
and against which the nation has come to
stand in so extreme an opposition.

These things are of the future and the
future is veiled from man.

I now leave this profound matter and
resume my survey of the writer.

The main points of what I have to say

in my fragment upon the conditions of survival in Gilbert Chesterton's writings, may be tabulated as follows:

I. The leading characteristic of Chesterton as a writer and as a man (the two were much more closely identified in him than in most writers) was that he was *national*.

I will point out in a moment what the effects of this were upon his treatment of various subjects.

II. The next characteristic was an extreme precision of thought, such as used to be characteristic of Englishmen, though in modern times it has broken down and people have forgotten how native it was to the English mind in the past.

III. The third characteristic I note about his writing and thought is a unique capacity for *parallelism*. He continually illumined and explained realities by com-

parisons. This was really the weapon peculiar to Chesterton's genius. It was the one
thing which he in particular had, and which
no one else in his time came near to, and
few in the past have approached. It is the
strongest element in his writing and thinking, after the far less exceptional element
of sincerity.

IV. The structure upon which his
work, like that of all modern men, had
been founded, was historical: but it was
only in general historical; it was far more
deeply and widely *literary*. (I believe I
notice this the more because with me it has
always been the other way about; I have a
very great deal of reading and experience
upon history, far less upon literature.)

V. Charity. He approached controversy, his delight, hardly ever as a conflict,
nearly always as an appreciation, including
that of his opponent.

VI. Lastly there is that chief matter of

his life and therefore of his literary activity, his acceptation of the Faith.

Let me now consider each of these six points separately.

I. Chesterton I say was national in every way it is possible for a writer and thinker to be national, or for a character to be national in private life apart from its public activity with pen or voice. It is one of the things, perhaps the main thing, in which Chesterton can be bracketed with the great character to whom he was so often compared: Samuel Johnson.

Often in his conversation with me I have noticed some colouring adjective or short phrase which showed how all his mind referred experience to national standards. Here, as in other matters, he drew from sources older and far stronger than the perversion of nationalism which had afflicted Englishmen more and more since his own youth.

The characteristic writer of this degraded mood is Kipling. With the mention of that name we are reminded of the opposing fates that confront the future of England. The two public writers that stand for these two tendencies are Kipling and Chesterton. Each is national—but in very different ways. Chesterton is national in himself. He is English of the English. To follow his mind and its expression is an introduction to the English soul. He is a mirror of England, and especially is he English in his *method* of thought, as he is in his understanding of things and men. He writes with an English accent.

Kipling has little about him of England or indeed of these islands. He has no sense of the English past or of the things natively and essentially English; he is rather of Asia and of the transplanted. But he is a representative of modern England through his enormous audiences. All that which we call today "The suburbs" is full of Kipling, and to Kipling the English urban middle class immediately respond. His verse especially appeals to it, far more than do his few powerful short stories.

All of us who have travelled can witness to the effect of Kipling upon the reputation of England abroad. Kipling's ignorance of Europe, his vulgarity and its accompanying fear of superiors (which modern people call an inferiority-complex) have profoundly affected and affected adversely the reputation of England and the Englishman throughout the world. This for two reasons:

(a) The fact that Kipling was un-English and Imperial threw him at once into contact with the New World, by which term I mean the United States of the Protestant tradition and Australasia.

(b) Fate would have it that Kipling should be translated into French by a genius, who makes him out in that language a far greater writer than he is. Now French being, after Latin, the universal language of civilised Western man, the Continent of Europe has approached Kipling and has been affected by him and has given him a reputation upon these lines.

Chesterton was the opposite of Kipling as a nationalist and conservative.* Because his family and individual traditions were of an older and far more cultured time than our own, he could not appeal either to the New World or to the Continental world in a way either could easily understand. Chesterton's work has never been *properly* translated into French, and three-quarters of the ideas he had to put forward, were so unfamiliar to foreigners that they could hardly be understood by them. His most concise and epigrammatic judgments are

* I do not use this word "conservative" in the silly and now obsolete sense of a Parliamentary Party but in its true sense: "Conservative of Tradition", especially of tradition social and national.

often taken as mere verbal exploits, and the half-educated and uncultured, who are of the stuff by which modern opinion is ruled, use of him the term "paradoxical", in that special meaning of their own which they give to this word, meaning "nonsense through contradiction"; not the original and cultured meaning of "paradox": "illumination through an unexpected juxtaposition".

This national character of Chesterton came out strongly in his appreciation of the English landscape. He had little experience of seafaring life; he saw the sea not from a deck but as it is seen from the land: from an English cliff. He was strongly impressed by its clean horizon and by its strength; even by the great voice of it, which is only heard when it comes in contact with its limits on the shore. But in this omission, as it were, of seafaring, he was more national than ever; for though the

English have a strong political and literary passion for the sea, they have as a people little personal familiarity with it, save on its shores. Thus you do not find among them the knowledge of the blind impersonal force of the sea which some have called the cruelty of the sea. Nor do you find among them a regard of the sea as the road to things *other* than themselves. The sea in the modern English mind is a road to commerce and to their colonial fellow subjects or administrators.

The nationalism of Chesterton was providential, not only for his own fame but for its effect upon his readers. It formed a bridge or link between the English mind as it has been formed by the Reformation (and particularly the later part of the Reformation, during the 17th century), and the general culture of Europe which was created by, and can only be preserved through, the Catholic Church.

Chesterton by his intellectual inheritance from the high Unitarian English culture was highly sympathetic with the general classical culture of Europe. He could illustrate it and pass it on (often unconsciously), as could not a writer or a man who knew not the soul of that culture. He could not have conceived a world which should be of our civilisation in a fashion and yet not based on Latin and Greek.

I remember, some years before he was received into the Church and before he ever visited America, his asking me, as one with a wide experience of the United States, whether it were true that the Latin and Greek classics were there of no effect. I told him this was increasingly so, save in a very few academic coteries and, of course, in the ubiquitous and very numerous Catholic clergy, and those influenced by them.

I had a private conversation with him walking in the lanes of Beaconsfield in

which he said to me, some two or three
years before being received into the Catholic Church, that an obstacle which always
presented itself to him was the alien character of the Faith in the eyes of a modern
Englishman. He said that I myself was
cosmopolitan in experience, for I had often
talked with him about the way in which I
had torn myself up by the roots in my
twentieth year and had gone all over
America by myself and had later undertaken the adventure of service in a foreign
army. Also I had a foreign name and certain ties of blood abroad.

I pointed out that among his intimate
acquaintance apart from myself was the
example of Maurice Baring. He answered
with justice that Maurice Baring also was
cosmopolitan in his experience and outlook.
"What I want,"he said (I recall his exact
words, for they made a profound impression on me), "is some-one entirely English

who should none the less have come in."
The objection is one that has occurred to
all Englishmen in a spiritual crisis of this
kind. It is inevitable.

I may conclude this point by repeating
that the *national* character of Chesterton
is strongly marked in his style. The con-
struction of his paragraphs and the se-
quence of his reasoning is so thoroughly
national that efforts at translating him have,
as I have said above, failed. I also here
repeat that if he had been less national
foreign nations of the Catholic culture
would be more familiar with him to-day
than they are.

One example of this national character
and style is the way in which the word
suggests the word in his writing: a thing
not unconnected with the effect of the Jac-
obean Bible on the English mind since the
17th century, particularly the Epistles of
St. Paul. Renan has remarked on this characteristic in the Epistles. It is in this con-

nection that the frequent use of puns, or, when they are not puns, plays upon words in Chesterton's writings, should be noted.

Lastly, there is the national character of high individualisation, which some have also called "localisation"; the preference of concrete connotation to abstraction. Chesterton is in the full tradition of those creative English writers from Chaucer to Dickens, who dwell not upon ideas but upon men and women, and especially is he national in his vast survey of English letters, where of Kipling is wholly ignorant.*

II. I have said that the second leading characteristic of Chesterton's mind and

* He who would judge the *Nationalism*, the "Englishry" of Chesterton's mind in contrast with the "Imperialism," the un-English tone of Kipling's should contrast their drawings as well as their writings. Chesterton's innumerable drawings of human expression are quintessentially English, distilled and double distilled English. Kipling's efforts in this line are as decadent as the French Latin quarter of a lifetime ago, or as Aubrey Beardsley's exact and poisonous line.

habit of writing is precision in reasoning. Many might superficially say that this talent clashed with his nationalism and was even contradictory thereto. I cannot agree.

The English, even the modern English, formed by the Reformation, have excelled in precision of thought. You see it in their vast volume of deduction in law, comparable to that of no other nation. You see it also in their special department of economics—a science which one may say was created in England.

This highly English tendency to precision has intellectual drawbacks as well as intellectual advantages, though the advantages can hardly be exaggerated. One drawback lies in this: that a man having exactly defined his terms and noted the weakness of an opponent's argument from the use of the same word in various senses, tends to verbalism. He is always in some danger of missing an opponent's just conclusions, when these have been arrived at from erroneous premises.

All thought is deductive. The opposition of "induction" to "deduction" is but verbal jingle. Induction is not thought at all. We have it in common with the animals. It is mere experiment and observation. Strictly speaking, when you think out a conclusion, that process must be deductive. For that very reason, you must be certain before you establish your conclusion firmly that your premises are sufficient. Now no premises other than the mathematical are wholly universal. So true is this that modern sophists have even sunk to attempting the reconciliation of contradictories. Great havoc have they made with this folly.

Take it by and large, Chesterton's passion for precision of thought was an overwhelming advantage for him over all his modern opponents in controversy, especially for his modern opponents of English speech, or rather of Protestant English culture.

In theology, for instance, he excluded Modernism with the nearest approach to contempt that a mind of such wide sympathy could achieve. He was impatient of all ambiguous nonsense, but it was in his nature to leave it aside rather than to transfix it with ridicule or invective. Had he indulged more in the latter, it is my judgment that his effect would have been stronger and perhaps more permanent: for it has been well said that the fame and effect of a man are buttressed by his enemies. As I shall come to say when I speak of his spiritual virtue, he made no enemies.

This habit of precision in thought and diction made of Chesterton a sort of what the French call a *revenant* on the highest phase of European and Christian thought. A *revenant* is one who comes back, one who reappears. Unfortunately, it also means a ghost. If you exemplify in your mind and also in your style an intellectual perfection which your contemporaries have lost, you will be a *revenant* and in danger of having less effect on those contemporaries. Although Chesterton's precision of thought and supreme talent for exact logic had much to do with his failure to conduct the mind of his contemporaries, he did influence that mind through the emotions. For indeed, his contemporaries of the Protestant culture live upon emotion and know of hardly any other process for arriving at conviction.

Fools are fond of repeating in chorus that the English are not a logical nation. They might as well say that the Italians are not an artistic nation, nor the Spaniards a soldierly nation. The English have been the special masters of logic in the past and still use it with a razor-like edge in circum-

scribed contemporary discussion, as you
may see any day by listening to the plead-
ings in an English law-court, or by reading
any one of the principal arguments advanced for theories in physical science by
the English discoverers of the 19th century
such as the great Huxley.

What men mean when they say that the
English are not a logical nation is that
nothing in their modern education makes
them familiar with logic in the largest
matters, whether these be political or the
supreme matters of religion. It is a weakness, for with politics especially, but also
with religion on its moral and practical
side, an error in first premises is usually
disastrous.

Thus you may predicate as a first principle the equality of man, which is an abso-
lutely certain truth: men are only men by
the qualities they have in common with
their fellows. But unless you (a) get the

term in its exact meaning and (b) supplement it by other equally certain general principles, you might be led into such absurdities as thinking that the two sexes have similar aptitudes for public life, or regarding the inexperienced as equally wise with the experienced, or denying the effect of wealth on the opportunities for acquiring experience and manners.

One effect of Chesterton's unique and exceptional precision of thought is the peculiar satisfaction his writing gives to men of philosophical training or instinct. But I use the word "philosophical" here to mean the search for truth in the reasonable hope of attaining it; not a contemptible shilly-shally of opinion, or the still more contemptible practice of advocacy in defence of all theories or of none.

Men who are accustomed to the terse and packed rational process of the past, and particularly to the master mind of St.

Thomas, will always eagerly seek a page of exposition from the pen of Gilbert Chesterton. But men who cannot taste a truth unless it be highly seasoned with epigram and shock, will misunderstand his manner, because it will satisfy them for the wrong reason. Chesterton is perpetually pulling up the reader with a shock of surprise, and his pages are crammed with epigram. Neither the one nor the other is the heart of his style. The heart of his style is lucidity, produced by a complete rejection of ambiguity: complete exactitude of definition.

While there is in this, as I have said, a peril to his contemporary effect and to its permanence in one way, because he wrote in the English tongue and for a public melted into the last dilution of English Protestantism—a public therefore which was almost physically incapable of appreciating precision in the major matters of life—there is, on the other hand, a strong chance of permanence in another way. For your precise thinker stands unchanged: unaffected by the fluctuations of fashion in expression.

Here, as in many other connections, the permanent effect of Gilbert Chesterton's writing must largely depend upon our return or non-return to the high culture which we have lost. This means in practice the return or non-return of England to the Catholic Church. The English-speaking public, apart from the Irish race, is now Protestant. It has been strongly and increasingly Anti-Catholic for now 250 years. Through the effect of time it is to-day more soaked in Protestantism than ever it was before.

Here, as in every other matter, the permanence of Chesterton's fame will depend upon that very doubtful contingency—the conversion of England.

III. I have said that parallelism was the weapon peculiar to Chesterton's genius.

His unique, his capital, genius for illustration by parallel, by example, is his peculiar mark. The word "peculiar" is here the operative word. Many have precision, though few have his degree of precision. Multitudes, of course, are national in their various ways. No one whatsoever that I can recall in the whole course of English letters had his amazing—I would almost say superhuman—capacity for parallelism.

Now parallelism is a gift or method of vast effect in the conveyance of truth.

Parallelism consists in the illustration of some unperceived truth by its exact consonance with the reflection of a truth already known and perceived.

A truth may be missed by too constant a use, so that familiarity has dulled it; or by mere lack of acquaintance with it (the opposite danger); or by the repeated statement of it in false and imperfect forms. When the truth has been missed, it is recalled and fixed in the mind of the hearer by an unexpected and vivid use of parallelism.

Whenever Chesterton begins a sentence with, "It is as though," (in exploding a false bit of reasoning,) you may expect a stroke of parallelism as vivid as a lightning flash. Thus if some ass propounds that a difference of application destroys the validity of a doctrine, or that particulars are the enemies of universals, Chesterton will answer: "It is as though you were to say I cannot be an Englishman because I am a Londoner," or "It is as though you were to say that I cannot be an Englishman because I travel," or "As though you were to say Brown and Smith cannot both be Englishmen because one of them talks West Country and the other North Country."

This invaluable instrument of exposition, parallelism, you will find enshrined in metaphor; and in metaphor (or in its parent, simile) Chesterton also excelled. But he was at his greatest and most forcible when he fully developed the method through open and *explicit* parallelism.

He introduces it in more than one form; with the phrase I have just quoted, "It is as though," or more violently, the phrase "Why not say while you are about it," followed by an example of the absurdity rebuked.

For instance, to one who said all concealment was falsehood, he would reply: "Why not say, *while you are about it, that* 'Wearing clothes is a falsehood?' "

Sometimes he would use the form, "What should we think of a person who might say?" Sometimes he left out exordium altogether and merely stated the parallelism without addition. Always, in whatever manner he launched the parallelism, he produced the shock of illumination. He *taught*.

He made men see what they had not seen

before. He made them *know*. He was an architect of certitude, whenever he practised this art in which he excelled.

The example of the parable in Holy Writ will occur at once to the reader. It is of the same origin and of similar value. The "parable" of the Gospels differs only from pure parallelism in the artifice of introducing a story in order to capture the reader's mind. But in essence a parable is the same thing as a parallelism.

Let us remark in conclusion that parallelism is of particular value in a society such as ours which has lost the habit of thinking. It illustrates and thereby fixes a truth or an experience as a picture fixes a face or landscape in the mind.

It is (alas!) unlikely that this invaluable instrument will be so used again by any other; but Chesterton has used it to perfection and in abundance.

It permeated not only his vigorous expository prose, but still more his private conversation. How well I recall the discussions upon all affairs, of art, of politics, of philosophy, in which this genius of his appeared! All he advanced as argument was lit up by the comparison of an unknown by a known truth; of something half hidden by something fully experienced among us all.

Parallelism was so native to his mind; it was so naturally a fruit of his mental character that he had difficulty in understanding why others did not use it with the same lavish facility as himself.

I can speak here with experience, for in these conversations with him or listening to his conversation with others I was always astonished at an ability in illustration which I not only have never seen equalled, but cannot remember to have seen attempted. He never sought such things; they poured out from him as easily as though they were not the hard forged products of intense vision, but spontaneous remarks.

I know what I am talking about. Over and over again I have myself attempted to make something clear to my fellows by sharp, exact and revealing parallel. I have always had to seek long before I found anything approaching what I needed and the thing itself I never found. I have never been able to form a parallel which could satisfy my desire for illustration; and even metaphor, in which my contemporaries abound, I have, by a sort of instinct, avoided: perhaps because I was not competent therein: perhaps from scorn.

For it must be noted that metaphor lends itself to abuse. I remember the good laugh which Chesterton and I had together over the opening words of a politically-minded Anglican Bishop speaking on some tawdry public occasion. The prelate had been badly bitten, probably in youth (perhaps in the days of Cecil Rhodes, William Stead and the more valuable Mahan), by Oceanic visions. He opened his speech, which was almost a sermon, with the phrase, "Let us strengthen while we loosen the bonds of Empire."

We both heard these words together and they became deathless in each of our memories, as the example of how to talk nonsense which will go down.

Thus, if England were attacked by a savage foe determined to annihilate her commerce and destroy her wealth, and a Dominion were to open the ball by proclaiming its neutrality in the war, that would be an excellent result of what we have been doing for the last lifetime: strengthening the bonds of Empire by loosening them. We shall probably have a complete example of it in the near future.

The original of the metaphor is obvious. You can strengthen the attachment of a boat to its moorings by paying out rope to

avoid too taut a strain; but to use that metaphor as an argument for slipping your
moorings altogether, as has been done with
the Dominions, would be folly.

In so far as this supreme gift of parallelism lessened Chesterton's reputation with
his contemporaries, instead of enhancing it
as it should have done, it so lessened his
reputation because his contemporaries were
warped by the pestilent habit of advocacy.

Advocacy is the chief political disease
of Englishmen to-day. They have pushed it
so far that they excuse the basic immorality
of legal chicanery by talking of "the law-
yer's duty to his client." And every single
one of our public questions is argued
threadbare, not with a desire to reach truth,
but with the desire to excel in forensic debate, which has become with us a rooted
and universal decadent habit.

Now for advocacy Gilbert Chesterton
had all his life not only an invincible re-
pulsion but an inability to be attracted by

it; or even to use it. In his early youth he enjoyed mere debate, and has told me of his experiences in this. But long before maturity, when he was still a young man, indeed, from the moment I first knew him—in his twenty-seventh year—he had done with it as a man has done with the toys of childhood.

Others all around him played with those toys all their lives—usually for pay: as leader-writers; as politicians; as humbugs of every kind. *He* remained fixed in his integrity.

IV.   My next point is Chesterton's *historical* basis.

All men who are interested in public affairs, but especially those who desire to influence such affairs, must concern themselves with two intellectual activities: History, without which one cannot understand

mankind or one's own times and people;
Literature, which is the expression of conscious and reasoning mankind.

Gilbert Chesterton, having for his supreme interest the business and fate of his
own country and of Christendom, occupied
himself with history and literature, as supports and nourishment to the philosophy
which it was his main business to expound.

Of these two departments, he was much
better grounded in literature than in history; and he had a far wider field of action
in literature than in history. The English
society in which he grew up—that of the
public schools and the social classes formed
by them—is not taught history seriously at
all. This defect attached to all the English
world during his career; and the same defect attaches to English teaching now.
There is no sign that it will be remedied.

Instinctively modern Englishmen have
only thought of history as a department of

politics; they desire only such history to be taught (if you can call it history at all) which shall strengthen the State or at least make its citizens feel self satisfied.

Thus certain national figures, like the pirates Drake and Hawkins, were set up as idols. The names mixed with isolated stories of occasional petty victories, especially naval, were repeated. The general development of Europe was left aside, and England was hardly regarded as part of that development. It was—and is—rare to meet an educated Englishman to-day who is familiar with the main lines of religious history on which all the rest is founded. The portentous revolution of the fourth and fifth centuries, whereby Christendom was established, is never seen in its magnitude, nor even in its character. The next most important event, the disruption of Christendom in the sixteenth and seventeenth centuries, is not grasped, in modern

England, because the Catholic Church, which was the matter of the tragedy, is not known there. The Catholic Culture is to the Englishman of to-day a foreign country.

From these inhibitions Gilbert Chesterton in a large measure freed himself. By right instinct and speech with the right men he guessed what Europe had been and filled in with right proportion the pitifully faint and imperfect (but above all *false*) outline which our modern books give to young men upon the past.

Thus some of his finest verse was historical and the history therein was just, with a particular appreciation of the defence of Christendom against the barbarian and the Mahommedan. No one else but Gilbert Chesterton could have written such a poem as *Lepanto* in English, and no one has attempted it; while the *Ballad of the White Horse* is an extension of the same theme.

He had a very strong appreciation of

what the Industrial Revolution had been and of how it warped the democratic revolution which might have led to a free peasantry here as it did in other countries.

But his triumph (if I may so call it), in the historical field was his appreciation of Ireland. No other English writer has come near to Chesterton in understanding both the nature of Ireland and the overwhelming importance of the Irish in the English story.

His treatment of the whole Irish question was, from the beginning, after he first became fully acquainted with it, that of a man who really understands the historical origins and historical consequences of three historical things. (1) The conflict between tribal and feudal in the Middle Ages; (2) the far more fundamental conflict between Catholic and Anti-Catholic from the mid-sixteenth to the end of the seventeenth centuries; (3) the failure of hostile forces to

destroy Ireland in the eighteenth and nineteenth centuries. Yes, their failure; for although that destruction was very nearly ac-
complished in the climax of the Irish
Famine Ireland rose from the dead.

He was almost the only writing man
with a sufficient English public who knew
(to take one particular point) the volume
and decline of the Irish seafaring trade; or
(to take another, larger point) the fact that
all domestic Irish history after 1700 turns
on the effort persistently undertaken by the
Irish to recover property in their own soil.
They had been dispossessed at the end of
the seventeenth century—not two lifetimes
before the days in which his own parents
and their generation had lived. They have
recovered it by indomitable tenacity and
enduring political purpose in spite of ruin
and exile. What writer among us except
Chesterton understood that enormous thing
or its effect on the fate of England herself?

Read what he wrote on St. Patrick's Bell at the Eucharistic Congress of Dublin: one of the most perfect passages in his works.

Finally, Chesterton understood historically what was meant by the word Rome.

He had the singular good fortune to escape the University. Had he gone to Cambridge, or worse still to Oxford, he would afterwards have had to unlearn laboriously a whole complex of bad history most imperfect and even more false than it was imperfect. As it was, he was able to go straight to the root of the matter and to interpret it to such of his fellow citizens as would listen—and they are but a very small proportion of the whole.

Still, on history he was not sufficiently grounded; though the just perspective which nearly all his contemporaries lacked was his. In that perspective he understood for instance, the nations of Catholic culture, and particularly, after Ireland, France.

It was remarkable that he should possess

this general view of the European Past for most of his English contemporaries had no such acquaintance with it. General history is not taught in England to-day and if taught would hardly be understood.

So much for history in the making of an English man of letters; he had vision of it: no more. But in English literature pure and simple he had an acquaintance very wide, accurate and, what is of more moment, critical. His first essay in this department was, I believe, the book on Robert Browning; but after that, in a mass of articles and books and in a myriad allusions and comments, coming in as it were from the side, he expounded English letters perpetually and at large.

Everything he wrote upon any one of the great English literary names was of the first quality. He summed up any one pen (that of Jane Austen, for instance) in exact sentences; sometimes in a single sentence, after a fashion which no one else has approached. He stood quite by himself in this department. He understood the very minds (to take the two most famous names) of Thackeray and of Dickens. He understood and presented Meredith. He understood the supremacy in Milton. He understood Pope. He understood the great Dryden. He was not swamped as nearly all his contemporaries were by Shakespeare, wherein they drown as in a vast sea—for that is what Shakespeare is. Gilbert Chesterton continued to understand the youngest and latest comers as he understood the forefathers in our great corpus of English verse and prose. It was a feat the more remarkable because all that corpus is conditioned by the Reformation, from the ethic and general philosophy of which he differed more and more as his life proceeded.

On this account, from his very profound science and vision came a difficulty in obtaining sufficient appreciation. He ought to be regarded as by far the best, almost the only, surveyor of that wide field. But in all that field the fine judgments he made were out of tune with what nine out of ten English audiences had taken for granted all their lives.

Nevertheless, his influence in explaining English letters to Englishmen was great, though perpetually frustrated. He was here a teacher who should have led but who was not permitted to lead. However, he was a teacher who was more listened to than if he had expended the same energy on, and had acquired the same voluminous acquaintance with, history.

It is thus that I see his principal advantage and disadvantage for the acquirement of permanent future fame. I for my part, who suffer from a singular ignorance of English literature, learnt most of what I know from him, but more from the benefit of his conversation even than from his writing. It is through him that I know what little I know of English fiction and prose in its right proportion. With English verse I can claim a better acquaintance.

V. Chesterton's connection with the Faith is much the most important aspect of his literary life, and deserves more detailed treatment than any other part of his activities. I have already dealt with its general character. I would now like to deal with it in more detail as a special department of any rational enquiry into the work and effect of this great man.

Here I must begin by a statement so unusual that my readers may well think it extravagant. But unless that statement is made at the very beginning of this division all judgement on the man and his work falls out of proportion. This preliminary statement is an affirmation that the Catholic Church, its Creed and Doctrine, its action upon human life, its whole function is beyond comparison the most important fact not only in European history but in the modern world to-day.

My contemporaries are quite unfamiliar with this piece of common sense. All the more reason for insisting upon it.

Here an important distinction must be made between the importance of a religion and its *truth*. I suppose ninety-nine English-men out of a hundred (including the greater part of that very small body which is both English by race and Catholic by religion) will regard my affirmation here as a mere personal opinion and distorted at that. "The writer is himself a Catholic," they will say, "and therefore gives to the Catholic Faith and practice an importance which is not to be discovered in the real world. The Catholic Church is but one of many things in the society around us; to give it this overwhelming and unique value is to exaggerate absurdly its place and function. No one could hold such a view unless he accepted himself the Faith and doctrine in question, and to propound it for the acceptance of other men is ridiculous."

That, I say, is certainly the way in which nearly all Englishmen would regard the judgement that the Catholic Faith is the dominating fact, not only in the history of Europe (and therefore of the world) but in our own contemporary society.

Yet so it is; and by the extent to which a man recognises that truth you may test his knowledge or his ignorance upon the things of the present or the past. *But the recognition of such a fact has nothing to do with the truth or falsehood of the Catholic claims.* The Church claims to be in exclusive possession of the only philosophy which explains man's place in the Universe, reveals man's relation with his Creator and gives him a rational account of his own nature. Therefore Her Doctrine is absolute and in Her eyes unquestionable.

But that claim is far from being universally accepted, it is, for the greater part of men, even in this European civilisation of ours which was moulded by the Faith, inadmisible.

Granted. It is in the nature of things that such a claim must sound monstrous to all those who reject it. But that has nothing to do with the importance of the institution which makes the claim. Those minds (in this country the great majority) who can hardly conceive that the claim exists and who certainly never connect the Catholic Church with any universal philosophy are fundamentally ignorant. They do not know the world they are living in. They do not see things are they are.

As an example of such ignorance, you may take the common insistence upon race as the chief factor in human society. Those who advance the proposition that race determines everything are talking without a knowledge of their subject. Race is an important factor in the development of human things and of social arrangements, but it is not the dominant or central factor. The dominant and central factor is, and must always be, an accepted scheme of values, especially of moral values. And such schemes we call religions.

Those who understand pubic affairs even less than do the racialists will ascribe to nationality the same overwhelming role which the racialists attach to race. They are even more wrong than the racialists, for a common nationality does not bind men save where the nation is enshrined as an idol to be worshipped by all.

There are many who take up an even less intelligent position than do the nationalists, and who make their test nothing more fundamental than mere language. These will talk of "Anglo-Saxons" or "The English-speaking world". Such people may be earnestly recommended to travel.

When you go about the world and see men as they are, when you watch their groupings and what are called to-day their "reactions", you soon discover that the lines of cleavage among them follow the lines of religion: not necessarily of religion conscious and expressed, but of ultimate religious training and formation.

Your popular writer on political matters is not only ignorant of this but is at some pains to substitute false terms for the true ones. Rather than talk of Catholic and Protestant cultures in Europe, for instance, he will talk of Teutons and Latins. And his readers are at least as much out of touch with reality as himself—otherwise he would not be a popular writer. The man who perceives, defines and extends truth by the pen is more likely to be an *un*popular writer.

There is a test immediately to hand by which we may judge the place of the

Church in human society. It is an ephemeral test but a striking one. It is the test of war and peace.

Even the most cretinous must by now perceive that modern war may be the destruction of all our world. In terror at that prospect men seek remedies for the chaos or defences against it. The most absurd of such experiments was, I suppose, the so-called "League of Nations" which left Islam out of account and yet gave sovereign authority to Abyssinia. It was founded on a silly falsehood and was unworthy of the mighty fruit it has produced—which is no less than the mortal peril wherein we now stand.

Others would seek a defence against this peril of death by setting up one power stronger than the rest to be the universal master over all. Mr. Christopher Hollis, for instance, who is justly prominent among those who discuss international matters, has suggested (in a very remarkable article* to which too much attention can hardly be paid) that the natural candidate for such a paramount position in modern Prussianised Germany, on account of its numbers, its disciplined unity and what is called its "efficiency"—that is its reduction of human activity to mechanics. Others have dreamt of a European unity to be restored in the Roman tradition, and this is the noble part of the Fascist extravagance. Others would prefer to live under the despotism of Moscow, enjoying all the delights and variety of Communism. Others more old-fashioned sigh for a strict alliance between Great Britain and the United States who should enjoy between them the domination of the world.

All these various reformers and Utopians

* The article here alluded to appeared in the London weekly newspaper *Truth* in the number published on Thursday, July 25th, 1940.

GILBERT CHESTERTON

omit what should surely be, according to all human experience, the one necessary spiritual foundation for unity, and that is *a common religion.*

This enormous omission, this flying in the face of common sense, may be excused in men and women who suffer from a general lack of experience and can conceive of no moral atmosphere save that which they breathed in early youth. Thus it has been very justly remarked of Mr. H. G. Wells (the most representative English writer of our time) that he is a Bible Christian who has lost his God. It may be similarly remarked of almost any common radical French politician taken at random from the rubbish heap of the now ruined French parliament that he is an anti-Catholic Catholic who has lost his Catholicism, and the same is true of fellow Masons in Rome and Madrid. It is strange but informing to discover that these wretchedly provincial attitudes of mind always think themselves universal, and nothing surprises world reformers of such a sort more than the discovery that other men differ from them. They are sure the benighted fellows can be easily set right by another little bout of propaganda.

Now it is, or should be, self-evident that a religion accepted as universal settles the quarrel and it is the only conceivable force that can do so: hence the overwhelming interest which all reasonable men should attach to the religion which so proposes to be universal.

That one of Chesterton's innumerable pieces of work wherein the effect of the Faith is most evident is also his best piece of work. Of all his books it is by far the most profound and the most clear, and for my part I should like to make it a test of any man's critical sense to have him take up that last volume of Essays, not the very last, I think, but among the last which he published and which was given to the world under the title of "The Thing".*

"The Thing" first appeared nearly eleven years ago in the Autumn of 1929. I am curious and even meditative upon its probable fate. If it is read by the generation now rising, that will mean that England is beginning to think. If it is forgotten, that will mean that thought is failing; for nowhere has there been more thorough thinking or clearer exposition in our time.

To illustrate this I will break my general rule and admit a quotation from what is perhaps the chief essay in a work crowded with intellectual triumphs. I refer to the essay which bears the plain title "Why I am a Catholic":

---

* The reader may find the book in small convenient form reprinted by its original publishers, Messrs. Sheed & Ward, in their Unicorn Library.

"I would undertake to pick up any topic at random, from pork to pyrotechnics, and show that it illustrates the truth of the only true philosophy; so realistic is the remark that all roads lead to Rome. Out of all these I have here only taken one fact; that the thing is pursued age after age by unreasonable hatred that is perpetually changing its reason. Now of nearly all the dead heresies it may be said that they are not only dead, but damned; that is, they are condemned or would be condemned by common sense, even outside the Church, when once the mood and mania of them is passed. Nobody now wants to revive the Divine Rights of Kings which the first Anglicans advanced against the Pope. Nobody now wants to revive the Calvinism which the first Puritans advanced against the King. Nobody now is sorry that the Iconoclasts were prevented from smashing all the statues of Italy. Nobody now is sorry that the Jansenists failed to destroy all the dramas of France. Nobody who knows anything about the Albigensians regrets that they did not convert the world to pessimism and perversion. Nobody who really understands the logic of the Lollards (a much more sympathetic set of People) really wishes that they had succeeded in taking away all political rights and privileges from everybody who was not in a state of grace. "Dominion founded on Grace" was a devout ideal; but considered as a plan for disregarding an Irish policeman controlling the traffic in Piccadilly, until we have discovered whether he has confessed recently to his Irish priest, it is wanting in actuality. In nine cases out of ten the Church simply stood for sanity and social balance against heretics who were sometimes very like lunatics. Yet at each separate moment the pressure of the prevalent error was very strong; the exaggerated error of a whole generation, like the strength of the Manchester School in the 'fifties, or of Fabian Socialism as a fashion in my own youth. A study of the true historical cases commonly shows us the spirit of the age going wrong, and the Catholics at least relatively going right. It is a mind surviving a hundred moods.

As I say, this is only one aspect; but it was the first that affected me and it leads on to others. When a hammer has hit the right nail on the head a hundred times, there comes a time when we think it was not altogether by accident. But these historical proofs would be nothing without the human and personal proofs, which would need quite a different sort of description. It is enough to say that those who know the Catholic practice find it not only right, but always right when everything else is wrong; making the Confessional the very throne of candour where the world outside talks nonsense about it as a sort of conspiracy; upholding humility when everybody is praising pride; charged with sentimental charity when the world is talking a brutal utilitarianism; charged with dogmatic harshness when the world is loud and loose with vulgar sentimentalism—as it is to-day. At the place where the roads meet there is no doubt of the convergence. A man may think of all sorts of things, most of them honest and many of them true, about the right way to turn in the maze at Hampton Court. But he does not think he is in the centre; he knows."

An excerpt never does justice to a writer. Least of all can an excerpt do justice to anything from the great flood of Chestertonian invention. His mind was oceanic, subject indeed to a certain restriction of repeated phrase and manner, but in no way restricted as to the action of the mind. He swooped upon an idea like an eagle, tore it with active beak into its constituent parts and brought out the heart of it. If ever a man analysed finally and conclusively Chesterton did so.

It was, I think, this in him, the intellectual dynamic action, which made it so difficult for his sluggish and superficial contemporaries to understand him. It would have been better perhaps had he never fallen into verbalism (wherein he tended to exceed). For fools were led thereby to think that he was merely verbalist whereas he was in reality a thinker so profound and so direct that he had no equal.

Anyhow, verbalist he was. It was his superficial defect and on that point I would like for a moment to linger.

God knows I do not use the term "verbalist" in derogation of his expression. I should be more proud than I can say if I could even have approached his clarity of speech, wherein he had but one rival, I think, Mr. H. G. Wells. But there is this difference between the two men: Chesterton had great things to say, while poor Wells never had anything to say, only other people's nothings to repeat.

Chesterton, being verbalist, was in most of his books (of Essays at least) perpetually punning. Now the teachers of the human race often exceeded in the direction of punning. The fathers of the Church were always at it (among whom I may quote the old tag *"Non est mendacium sed mysterium"*—which is, I believe, St. Augustine. Let me also quote *"Mutans Evae Nomen"*. I spare you five hundred others).

To revel in words is the mark of a master of words. The great Rabelais will nod and approve this verdict from his throne in heaven. It is no wonder that Chesterton in his magnificent exuberance should exceed where words were concerned and therefore fall into punning, which trope is based upon the word suggesting the word. But I always wish, when I am reading him, that he had avoided the temptation and had concentrated upon direct expression, wherein, like his contemporary H. G. Wells, he was a master.

Now let me turn to something else in the weighing of this genius. That he was exuberant we know. That he was profoundly English we know. That he loved to discover and to propound truth (the high task of a man!) we also know. That he had a unique capacity for propounding truth (usually, alas! to men who did not understand what they were hearing) we also know. But there is another quality about him which should be remembered and will be tested also by the years as they pass. He had *universality.*

By this I mean that he understood all men (wherein also was rooted his charity, whereon I next touch) and in particular his countrymen who are after their fashion the most diverse as they are certainly the most united and the most humorous of European men.

It seems to me that Gilbert Chesterton at his baptism was visited by three fairies. Two good and one evil. The two good fairies were the Fairy of fecundity in speech, and the Fairy of wide appreciation. The bad fairy was struck dead as she entered the church—and serve her right. He was blessed in knowing nothing of the acerbities which bite into the life of writing men.

The life of writing men has always been, since our remote fathers engaged upon it in the high Greek world, a bitter business. It is notoriously accompanied, for those who write well, by poverty and contempt; or by fatuity and wealth for those who write ill. It is unrewarded in this world and probably in the next—(seeing, that those who write well do so with their backs

put up like spitting cats—witness the im-
mortal Swift).

The writing man, I say, is a most un-
happy beast of burden (and I know something about it) ; he bears upon his back for
conveyance to others the joys and consola-
tions, the visions that make life in this bad
world tolerable. But he may not enjoy them
himself any more than the donkey may
enjoy the vegetables that he bears to market.

Now Gilbert Chesterton enjoyed this
singular, this very happy fate, that, though
he was a writing man the bitterness of the
trade never approached him. He was spared
its ignominies and its trials, which are a
sort of martyrdom whereby the writer earns
fame—which is worth nothing. He himself
had something much more worth while,
called Virtue.

I have said nothing in this very short
essay to judge his verse. I have avoided it
for two reasons. First of all because I know

myself to be fastidious in the matter, secondly because time judges these things and the date is too recent. There is hardly one example, at least among contemporaries, of a man being praised for his verse during his own lifetime for the right reasons.

But I will say this about Chesterton's verse: that, while it suffered from being voluminous and therefore loose, it struck perpetually the inward note.

Here again I will quote:

"Our Lady stroked the tall live grass, as a man strokes his steed."

That is good stuff! That is inward stuff! That is stuff you don't get in Anthologies!

And again I will quote:

"Don John of Austria has gone by Alcala."

That is from *Lepanto,* and it is a trumpet call! But indeed the whole of that poem *Lepanto* is not only the summit of Chesterton's achievement in verse but the summit of high rhetorical verse in all our generation. I have said this so often that I am almost tired of saying it again, but I must continue to say it. People who cannot see the value of *Lepanto* are half dead. Let them so remain.

Well, what will be the harvest of all this? How much will remain to English letters from that great fertile flood of writing and of thinking (but especially of thinking) which made this man so exceptional in our time?

I would answer, that no one can tell. The result depends not upon him but upon his country. It may be that his country is in decline and will be unable to learn the great lesson. It may be that this country (which he so deeply loved and so exactly represented) will rise to things even greater than those of its great past. If it does so, Gilbert Chesterton's name will be among the first of English names. If it does not, he will be forgotten.

VI.   All men one may say, or very nearly all men, have one leading moral defect. Few have one leading Christian virtue. That of Gilbert Chesterton was unmistakably the virtue of Christian charity: a virtue especially rare in writing men, and rarest of all in such of them as have a pursuing appetite for controversy—that is, for bolting out the truth.

He loved his fellow-men. Through this affection, which was all embracing he understood the common man; and that virtue, which was so conspicuous in all his private life and broad river of daily speech, was both a strength and a weakness to his fame.

It was a strength because it gave him access to every mind; men will always listen to a friend; and so much was he a friend of all those for whom he wrote that all were prepared to listen, however much they were puzzled. I shall always remember how once in America a man said to me, a man who I believe had never seen Chesterton in the flesh: "When I read of his death I felt the shock one feels upon the loss of a daily and beloved acquaintance."

The drawback, however, of this virtue of charity as regards its action upon his fame was that it prevented the presence in what he wrote of that acerbity or "bite" which gives an edge or rather a spearhead to every effort at persuasion. It preserved him from enmities. He had no enemies; and in a society such as ours in Modern England, a society which above all demands comfort and ease, this gave him a universality of appeal but furnished no occasion for attack. You do not rise from the reading of one of Chesterton's appreciations with that feeling of being armed which you obtain from the great satirists and particularly from the masters of irony.

He wounded none, but thus also he failed to provide weapons wherewith one may wound and kill folly. Now without wounding and killing, there is no battle; and thus, in this life, no victory; but also no peril to the soul through hatred.

Of the personal advantage to himself of so great and all-pervading a charity, too much cannot be said; but I believe it to be a drag upon his chances of endurance upon paper—for what that may be worth—and it is worth nothing compared with eternal things. Christendom would seem to be now entering an ultimate phase in the struggle between good and evil, which is, for us, the battle between the Catholic Church and its opponents. In that struggle, those will stand out in the future most vividly who most provoked hostility. To his lasting advantage in the essential things of the spirit, of his own individual soul, he did not provoke it.

He was aided in the preservation of such serenity by the gradualness of the approach he made to the right side of the battle. His name and writings were already familiar before his conversion, to a general public, which had no idea of the Faith. They were thus familiar and accepted long before he threw down the last challenge by fully accepting the Creed, the Unity and the temporal disabilities of Catholic allegiance. He had before his reception acquired, as it were, a privileged position which permitted him to be still listened to after he had crossed that frontier of the Faith beyond which lies all that his fellow-countrymen oppose.

Herein he was blessed and may be justly envied by those who are condemned by their Faith to exclusion and exile. In the appreciation of a man rather than of a writer virtue is immeasurably more important that literary talent and appeal. For these last make up nothing for the salvation of the soul and for an ultimate association with those who should be our unfailing companions in Beatitude: the Great Company. Of that Company he now is; so that it is a lesser and even indifferent thing to determine how much he shall also be of the company, the earthly and temporal company, of the local and temporarily famous.

What place he may take according to that lesser standard I cannot tell, because many years must pass before a man's position in the literature of his country can be called securely established.

We are too near to decide on this. But because we are so near and because those (such as I who write this) who were his companions, knew him through his very self and not through his external activity, we are in communion with him. So be it. He is in Heaven.

LIST OF
CHESTERTON'S WORKS

The following list of the chief works of Chesterton, with the date of their first appearance in book form, is taken from the *Everyman's Library* edition of his stories, essays, and poems by courtesy of Messrs. J. M. Dent & Sons Ltd. A large proportion of them are collections of essays first contributed to various journals.

Greybeards at Play, 1900; *The Wild Knight*, 1900 (new ed. 1914); *The Defendant*, 1901; *Twelve Types*, 1902; *Robert Browning*, 1903; *G. F. Watts*, 1904; *The Napoleon of Notting Hill*, 1904; *The Club of Queer Trades*, 1905; *Heretics*, 1905; *Charles Dickens*, 1906; *The Man who was Thursday*, 1908; *All Things considered*, 1908; *Orthodoxy*, 1908; *George Bernard Shaw*, 1909; *Tremendous Trifles*, 1909; *The Ball and the Cross*, 1910; *What's Wrong with the World*, 1910; *Alarms and Discursions*, 1910; *William Blake*, 1910; *Appreciations and Criticisms of the Works of Charles Dickens*, 1911; *Innocence of Father Brown*, 1911; *The Ballad of the White Horse*, 1911; *Manalive*, 1912; *A Miscellany of Men*, 1912; *The Victorian Age in Literature*, 1913; *Magic*, 1913; *The Flying Inn*, 1914; *The Wisdom of Father Brown*, 1914; *The Crimes of England*, 1915; *Poems*, 1915; *Wine, Water, and Song*, 1915; *A Shilling for my Thoughts*, 1916; *A Short History of England*, 1917; *Irish Impressions*, 1919; *The New Jerusalem*, 1920; *The Superstition of Divorce*, 1920; *The Uses of Diversity*, 1920; *The Ballad of St. Barbara*, 1922; *Eugenics and Other Evils*, 1922; *The Man who knew Too Much*, 1922; *What I saw in America*, 1922; *Fancies versus Fads*, 1923; *Saint Francis of*

Assisi, 1923; *The End of the Roman Road*, 1924; *The Everlasting Man*, 1925; *The Superstitions of the Sceptic*, 1925; *Tales of the Long Bow*, 1925; *The Catholic Church and Conversion*, 1926; *The Incredulity of Father Brown*, 1926; *The Queen of Seven Swords*, 1926; *The Outline of Sanity*, 1926; *William Cobbett*, 1926; *The Judgment of Dr. Johnson*, 1927; *Robert Louis Stevenson*, 1927; *The Secret of Father Brown*, 1927; *Generally Speaking*, 1928; *The Sword of Wood*, 1928; *Do we agree?* (a debate with Bernard Shaw), 1928; *The Poet and the Lunatics*, 1929; *The Thing*, 1929; *Four Faultless Felons*, 1930; *The Resurrection of Rome*, 1930; *Come to think of It*, 1930; *Adventures in Dramatic Criticism*, 1931; *All is Grist*, 1931; *Christendom in Dublin*, 1932; *Chaucer*, 1932; *Sidelights on New London and Newer York*, 1932; *All I Survey*, 1933; *St. Thomas Aquinas*, 1933; *Avowals and Denials*, 1934; *The Scandal of Father Brown*, 1935; *The Coloured Lands*, 1938; *The End of the Armistice*, 1940.

Collected editions of the poems were published in 1927 and 1933, and a volume of introductions was published under the title of *G. K. C. as M.C.* in 1929. Although Chesterton's work has brought forth from time to time appreciations—though, more often, rejoiners—no full and serious estimate of it has yet been made.

Publisher's note to the new edition: Since the publication of Belloc's essay a considerable literature has appeared on Chesterton. The most thorough bibliography of Chesterton has been compiled in two volumes by John Sullivan: *G. K. Chesterton. A Bibliography.* 1958. London: University of London Press. New

York: Barnes and Noble; *Chesterton Continued. A Bibliographical Supplement.* 1968. London: University of London Press. New York: Barnes and Noble. See also Sullivan's ongoing "Chesterton's Bibliography Continued" series in *The Chesterton Review,* Vol. II, No. 1 (Fall–Winter, 1975–76), pp. 94–98; Vol. II, No. 2 (Spring–Summer, 1976), pp. 267–272.

Of this edition of

On the Place of Gilbert Chesterton in English Letters,

750 copies have been printed.

This copy is No.

202